Tammy's
Original/Gluten Free Holiday
Cookbook

TAMMY AIKEN

ISBN 978-1-953223-41-8 (paperback)

Copyright © 2020 by Tammy Aiken

All rights reserved. No part of this publication may be reproduced, distributed, or transmitted in any form or by any means, including photocopying, recording, or other electronic or mechanical methods without the prior written permission of the publisher. For permission requests, solicit the publisher via the address below.

Rushmore Press LLC
1 800 460 9188
www.rushmorepress.com

Printed in the United States of America

Contents

Introduction 5

Gluten Free & Dairy Free Non-Alcoholic Bacardi Margarita Cupcakes 6

Original Non-Alcoholic Bacardi Margarita Cupcakes 7

Gluten Free and Dairy Free Peanut Butter Cookies for No Bake Peanut Butter Pie 8

Original Peanut Butter Cookies For No Bake Peanut Butter Pie 10

Gluten free and Dairy Free Wintergreen Mint Candy 12

Original Wintergreen Mint Candy 13

Gluten Free & Dairy Free Chocolate Cherry Bites 14

Original Chocolate Cherry Bites 15

Gluten Free & Dairy Free Raspberry Candy 16

Original Raspberry Candy 17

Gluten Free & Dairy Free Pumpkin Spice Mini Cupcakes 18

Original Pumpkin Spice Mini Cupcakes 19

Gluten Free & Dairy Free Irish Mint Chocolate Chip Cupcakes 20

Original Irish Mint Chocolate Chip Cupcakes 22

Gluten Free & Dairy Free Chocolate Cake 24

Original Chocolate Cake 25

Gluten Free & Dairy Free Homemade Custard 26

Original Homemade Custard 27

Gluten Free & Dairy Free Chocolate Chip Coconut Cookies 28

Original Chocolate Chip Coconut Cookies 29

Gluten Free & Dairy Free Jaffa Cakes 30

Original Jaffa Cakes 31

Gluten Free and Dairy Free Christmas Sugar Cookies 32

Original Christmas Sugar Cookie 33

Gluten Free & Dairy Free Coconut Cupcakes 34

Original Coconut Cupcakes 35

Gluten Free & Dairy Free Red Velvet Cupcakes 36

Original Red Velvet Cupcakes 37

Gluten Free & Dairy Free Strudel Topping Mini Cinnamon Breads 38

Original Strudel Topping Mini Cinnamon Breads 39

Gluten Free & Dairy Free Snicker Doodle Cookies 40

Original Snicker Doodle Cookies 41

Gluten Free and Dairy Free Peanut Butter Cups 42

Original Peanut Butter Cups 43

Bonus Recipe For Gluten Free Turkey Gravy 44

Gluten Free and Dairy Free Chocolate Pudding or Hot Chocolate 45

Ingredient Information 46

Substitutions 49

Introduction

My Holiday cookbook is to help people with Celiac disease so they can be able to have Holiday desserts! Everyone gets a sweet tooth, my Holiday cookbook will take care of that sweet tooth you have. People that are lactose sensitivity can also enjoy my Holiday desserts. It's very important for everyone no matter who it is to join in on the Holiday desserts with their families. With this cookbook you can make the original desserts and the gluten and dairy free desserts for you and your family. How cool is that having the same desserts as your family and not feeling left out.

Happy Holidays Everyone

Gluten Free & Dairy Free Non-Alcoholic Bacardi Margarita Cupcakes

- 2 eggs
- 1 teaspoon Baker's Corner baking powder or Stop & Shop baking powder
- ¼ teaspoon Baker's Corner baking soda or Stop & Shop baking soda
- ½ cup granulated sugar
- ½ cup frozen Bacardi mixers non-alcoholic, Thaw before using
- ¼ cup canola oil
- 1 cup gluten free flour, (not the all purpose gluten free flour)
- cupcake liners

Preheat oven to 350 degrees. In a mixing bowl add eggs, baking powder, baking soda, sugar, Bacardi mix, oil, mix. Add all the flour and mix. Add a full ¼ cup of batter to each cupcake liner. Bake for 20 to 25 minutes.

Gluten Free & Dairy Free Non-Alcoholic Bacardi Margarita buttercream

- 4 cups confectionery sugar
- 1 stick & 2 tablespoons softened Earth Balance Vegan butter
- 4 to 5 tablespoons Bacardi mix
- 1/8 teaspoon Americolor gel green food coloring

In a mix bowl add sugar, butter, mixing on low speed adding the Bacardi mix slowly until you get a desired consistency. Add the food coloring mix on high for 20 seconds to make a light buttercream.

Original Non-Alcoholic Bacardi Margarita Cupcakes

- 2 eggs
- 1 teaspoon baking powder
- ¼ teaspoon baking soda
- ½ cup granulated sugar
- ½ cup frozen Bacardi mixers non-alcoholic, Thaw before using
- ¼ cup canola oil
- 1 cup all purpose flour
- cupcake liners

Preheat oven to 350 degrees. In a mixing bowl add eggs, baking powder, baking soda, sugar, Bacardi mix, oil, mix. Add all the flour and mix. Add a full ¼ cup of batter to each cupcake liner. Bake for 20 to 25 minutes.

Original Non-Alcoholic Bacardi Margarita Buttercream

- 4 cups confectionery sugar
- 1 stick & 2 tablespoons softened unsalted butter
- 4 to 5 tablespoons Bacardi mix
- 1/8 teaspoon Americolor gel green food coloring

In a mix bowl add sugar, butter, mixing on low speed adding the Bacardi mix slowly until you get a desired consistency. Add the food coloring mix on high for 20 seconds to make a light buttercream.

Gluten Free and Dairy Free Peanut Butter Cookies for No Bake Peanut Butter Pie

Cookies:

- 2 eggs
- 1 cup smooth gluten free peanut butter
- 1 teaspoon Bakers Corner baking soda or Stop & Shop baking soda
- 1 cup granulated sugar
- ½ cup light brown sugar
- 3 tablespoons softened Earth Balance Vegan butter
- 1/8 teaspoon sea salt
- 1 cup gluten free flour, (not a gluten free all purpose flour)
- 13x18 baking sheet

Preheat the oven to 350 degrees. In a mixing bowl add eggs, peanut butter, baking soda, sugar, light brown sugar, butter, salt and mix. Add the flour all at once mix until combined, spray a cookie sheet with Pam (original non stick cooking spray only). Take the cookie dough and spread this on the bottom of the cookie sheet. Bake for 20 to 25 minutes take out let cool completely.

Gluten Free or Gluten Free and Dairy Free Peanut Butter Pie Squares For a Crowd

Filling:

- 1 cup gluten free smooth peanut butter
- 8 ounces softened cream cheese or Tofutti cream cheese
- 1 ½ cups confectionery sugar
- 3 tablespoons unsweetened original almond milk
- 3 cups Cool whip, reserve 1 ½ cups or 3 cups Coco whip, reserve 1 ½ cups

In a mixing bowl add the peanut butter and cream cheese mix, add the sugar and milk mix until all is combined. Add 1 ½ cups of Cool whip or 1 ½ cups of Coco whip to the filling. Mix and spread the filling over the cool crust. Spread 1 ½ cups Cool whip or 1 ½ cups Coco whip that you reserved over the top. Put into the refrigerator to set up for 2 hours.

Tip: You can double the recipe if your having a lot of people. If you double the crust you will have a much thicker crust.

Note: The Coco whip does taste like coconut but using this for the peanut butter pie you cannot taste the coconut flavor. I use the coco whip all the time for this pie. You can make the ice cream but with the gluten free and dairy free filling the texture will be soft.

Original Peanut Butter Cookies For No Bake Peanut Butter Pie

Cookies:

- 2 eggs
- 1 cup smooth peanut butter
- 1 cup granulated sugar
- ½ cup light brown sugar
- 1 teaspoon baking soda
- 4 tablespoons softened unsalted butter
- 1/8 teaspoon sea salt
- 1 cup all purpose flour
- 13 x 18 baking sheet

Preheat the oven to 350 degrees. In a mixing bowl add eggs, peanut butter, baking soda, sugar, light brown sugar, salt and mix. Add the flour all at once mix until combined, spray a cookie sheet with a non stick cooking spray. Take the cookie dough and spread this on the bottom of the cookie sheet. Bake for 25 to 30 minutes. Take out let cool completely.

Original Peanut Butter Pie Squares For a Crowd

Filling:

- 1 cup smooth peanut butter
- 8 ounces softened cream cheese
- 1 ½ cups confectionery sugar
- 3 tablespoons 1% milk
- 3 cups cool whip, reserve 1 ½ cups

In a mixing bowl add the peanut butter and cream cheese mix, add the sugar and milk mix until all is combined. Add 1 ½ cups of cool whip to the filling, mix spread the filling over the cool crust then spread the 1 ½ cups of cool whip you reserved over the top.

Tip: You can double the recipe if your having a lot of people. If you double the crust you will have a much thicker crust. You can just make the filling add only 1 cup of cool whip to the filling put this in a container with a tight fitting lid put in the freezer overnight.

Gluten free and Dairy Free Wintergreen Mint Candy

- 1 cup gluten free & dairy free white baking chips
- 1/8 teaspoon wintergreen flavoring
- pinch of green food coloring

In a microwave bowl add the white baking chips, microwave for 30 seconds at a time. Stirring every 30 seconds until smooth add the flavoring and the food coloring stir in. You want a mint green color. Drop on a piece of wax paper with a teaspoon swirl to make the candy round. Put in the refrigerator for 20 minutes to set up.

Note: You can melt gluten free and dairy free semi-sweet chocolate and dip the candy into it. You can also use candy molds.

Original Wintergreen Mint Candy

- 1 cup white chocolate chips, melted
- 1/8 teaspoon wintergreen flavoring
- pinch of green food coloring

In a microwave bowl add the white baking chips, microwave for 30 seconds at a time. Stirring every 30 seconds until smooth add the flavoring and the food coloring stir in. You want a mint green color. Drop candy onto a piece of wax paper with a teaspoon. Put in the refrigerator for 20 minutes to set up.

Note: You can make any shape you want for these even candy molds would be good to. Even dipped in melted milk chocolate.

Gluten Free & Dairy Free Chocolate Cherry Bites

- 4 ounces softened Tofutti cream cheese
- 1 ½ tablespoons confectionery sugar
- 8 chopped Maraschino cherries, chopped into small pieces, pat with a paper towel
- 1 ¼ cups Enjoy Life-Semi-sweet chocolate chips, melted
- mini cupcake liners

In a small bowl add cream cheese, confectionery sugar, chopped cherries, mix, set aside. Add chocolate chips to the microwave bowl, microwave for 30 seconds at a time mixing in between until smooth. Take a cupcake liner add a ½ teaspoon of melted chocolate to the bottom of the cupcake liner spread on the bottom and up the sides. Take a full level teaspoon of the cherry mixture add to the center spread. Add a full teaspoon of melted chocolate over the top spread to cover all.

Gluten Free & Dairy Free Filling For Celery

- 1-8 ounce softened Tofutti
- 1 jar Maraschino cherries, chopped into small pieces, pat with a paper towel
- Add 1 teaspoon cherry juice at a time until you get thick consistency
- 1/3 cup confectionery sugar

In a mixing bowl add all ingredients and mix. If you like the filling sweeter just add more confectionery sugar a little at a time. This cherry filling is my Aunt Joanne's recipe for stuffed celery. I decided to make candy with the filling.

Note: This is your choice to try this with the Tofutti. The taste and texture will be different. Example: Maybe they like this with more cherry juice where you can actually dip the celery.

Original Chocolate Cherry Bites

- 4 ounces softened cream cheese
- 1 ½ tablespoons confectionery sugar
- 8 chopped Maraschino cherries, chopped into small pieces, pat with a paper towel
- 1 ¼ cups milk chocolate chips, melted
- mini cupcake liners

In a small bowl add cream cheese, confectionery sugar, chopped cherries, mix, set aside. Add chocolate chips to the microwave bowl, microwave for 30 seconds at a time mixing in between until smooth. Take a cupcake liner add a ½ teaspoon of melted chocolate to the bottom of the cupcake liner spread on the bottom and half way up the sides. Take a full level teaspoon of the cherry mixture add to the center spread. Add a full teaspoon of melted chocolate over the top spread to cover all.

Original Filling For Celery

- 1-8 ounce softened cream cheese
- 1 jar Maraschino cherries, chopped into small pieces, pat with a paper towel
- Add 1 teaspoon cherry juice at a time until you get thick consistency
- 1/3 cup confectionery sugar

In a mixing bowl add all ingredients and mix. If you like the filling sweeter just add more confectionery sugar a little at a time. This cherry filling is my Aunt Joanne's recipe for stuffed celery. I decided to make candy with the filling.

Note: Sometimes people like different consistencies. Example: Maybe they like this with more cherry juice where you can actually dip the celery.

Gluten Free & Dairy Free Raspberry Candy

- gluten free & dairy free white chocolate chip
- 1 ½ teaspoons raspberry extract
- pinch Americolor red food coloring
- 1 cup melted Enjoy Life Semi-sweet chocolate chips
- wax paper
- plate

Add the white chocolate to a microwave glass bowl. Put in the microwave for 30 seconds at a time. When looking like almost melted take out stir until smooth. Add the flavoring and food coloring mix this will get hard to mix you want it this way. Place wax paper on a plate shape the chocolate into 1 inch balls. Put in the refrigerator for 30 minutes to set up. Same directions for melting the chocolate chips as you melted the white chocolate chips. Dip the balls into the melted chocolate place back on the wax paper. Place in the refrigerator for 30 minutes to set up.

Note: You can make the color more a red for the raspberry.

Original Raspberry Candy

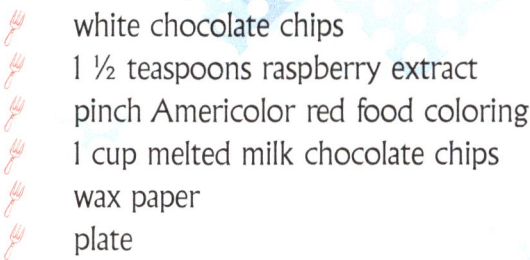

- white chocolate chips
- 1 ½ teaspoons raspberry extract
- pinch Americolor red food coloring
- 1 cup melted milk chocolate chips
- wax paper
- plate

Add the white chocolate to a microwave glass bowl. Put in the microwave for 30 seconds at a time. When looking like almost melted take out stir until smooth. Add the flavoring and food coloring mix this will get hard to mix you want it this way. Place wax paper on a plate shape the chocolate into 1 inch balls. Put in the refrigerator for 30 minutes to set up. Same directions for melting the chocolate chips as you melted the white chocolate chips. Dip the balls into the melted chocolate place back on the wax paper. Place in the refrigerator for 30 minutes to set up.

Note: You can make the color more a red for the raspberry.

Gluten Free & Dairy Free Pumpkin Spice Mini Cupcakes

- 2 eggs
- 1/3 cup canola oil
- ½ cup unsweetened original almond milk
- ½ cup 100% canned pumpkin
- 1 teaspoon ground cinnamon or Vietnamese ground cinnamon
- 1/8 teaspoon ground clove
- ¼ teaspoon ground ginger
- ½ teaspoon fresh grated nutmeg or ground nutmeg
- ¼ teaspoon Baker's Corner baking soda or Stop and Shop baking soda
- 1 teaspoon Baker's Corner baking powder or Stop and Shop baking powder
- ½ cup granulated sugar
- 1 cup gluten free flour, (not the all purpose gluten free flour)
- ½ cup chopped walnuts, optional
- mini cupcake liners

Preheat oven to 300 degrees. In a mixing bowl add eggs, oil, milk, pumpkin and all your spices. Add the baking soda, baking powder, sugar mix. Add all the flour and mix. Add a ½ tablespoon of batter to each cupcake liner. Bake for 20 to 25 minutes.

Gluten Free & Dairy Free Pumpkin Spice Buttercream

- 5 cups confectionery sugar
- 1 stick softened Earth Balance Vegan butter
- 1 teaspoon ground cinnamon or Vietnamese ground cinnamon
- 1/8 teaspoon ground clove
- ¼ teaspoon ground ginger
- ½ teaspoon fresh grated nutmeg or ground nutmeg
- 4 to 5 tablespoons unsweetened original almond milk

In a mixing bowl add all the sugar, butter, spices and mix. On low speed adding the milk a tablespoon at a time until you get the desired consistency. Mix on high for 20 seconds.

Note: You can freeze this buttercream up to two months if you have extra.

Original Pumpkin Spice Mini Cupcakes

- 2 eggs
- 1/3 cup canola oil
- ½ cup 1% milk
- ½ cup 100% canned pumpkin
- 1 teaspoon ground cinnamon or Vietnamese ground cinnamon
- 1/8 teaspoon ground clove
- ¼ teaspoon ground ginger
- ½ teaspoon fresh nutmeg or ground nutmeg
- ¼ teaspoon baking soda
- 1 teaspoon baking powder
- ½ cup granulated sugar
- ½ cups chopped walnuts, optional
- Mini cupcake liners

Preheat oven to 300 degrees. In a mixing bowl add eggs, oil, milk, pumpkin, all your spices mix. Add baking soda, baking powder, sugar and mix. Add ½ tablespoon of batter in each cupcake liner. Bake for 20 to 25 minutes.

Original Pumpkin Spice Buttercream

- 5 cups confectionery sugar
- 1 stick softened unsalted butter
- 1 teaspoon ground cinnamon or Vietnamese ground cinnamon
- 1/8 teaspoon ground clove
- ¼ teaspoon ground ginger
- ½ teaspoon fresh grated nutmeg or ground nutmeg
- 4 to 5 tablespoons 1% milk

In a mixing bowl add all the sugar, butter, spices and mix. On low speed adding the milk a tablespoon at a time until you get the desired consistency. Mix on high for 20 seconds.

Note: You can freeze this buttercream up to two months if you have extra.

Gluten Free & Dairy Free Irish Mint Chocolate Chip Cupcakes

- 2 eggs
- 1/3 cup canola oil
- ¼ teaspoon Irish mint flavoring
- ½ cup unsweetened original almond milk
- ¼ green gel food coloring
- ½ cup granulated sugar
- 1 teaspoon Baker's Corner baking powder or Stop & Shop baking powder
- ¼ teaspoon Baker's Corner baking soda or Stop & Shop baking soda
- 1 cup gluten free flour, (not the all purpose gluten free flour)
- ½ cup Enjoy Life Semi-sweet chocolate chips
- cupcake liners

Preheat the oven to 350 degrees. In a mixing bowl add eggs, oil, flavoring, milk, food coloring, sugar, baking powder, baking soda, mix. Add all the flour and mix. Add the chocolate chips mix in with a spoon. Add a full ¼ cup of batter to each cupcake liner. Bake for 25 to 30 minutes.

Gluten Free & Dairy Free Chocolate Irish Buttercream for Filling

- 4 cups confectionery sugar
- 2 sticks softened Earth Balance Vegan butter
- 3 tablespoons unsweetened cocoa
- ¼ teaspoon Irish mint flavoring
- 4 to 5 tablespoons unsweetened original almond milk

In a mixing bowl add sugar, butter, cocoa, flavoring, start to mix on low speed adding the milk a tablespoon at a time until you get a desired consistency.

Gluten Free & Dairy Free Irish Mint Buttercream for Top

- 9 cups confectionery sugar
- 2 sticks softened Earth Balance Vegan butter
- 1/8 teaspoon hobbyland Irish mint flavoring
- 1/8 teaspoon Americolor mint green gel food coloring
- 7 to 8 tablespoons unsweetened original almond milk

In a mixing bowl add sugar, butter, flavoring, food coloring, mix on low speed adding the milk a tablespoon at a time to get the desired consistency.

Original Irish Mint Chocolate Chip Cupcakes

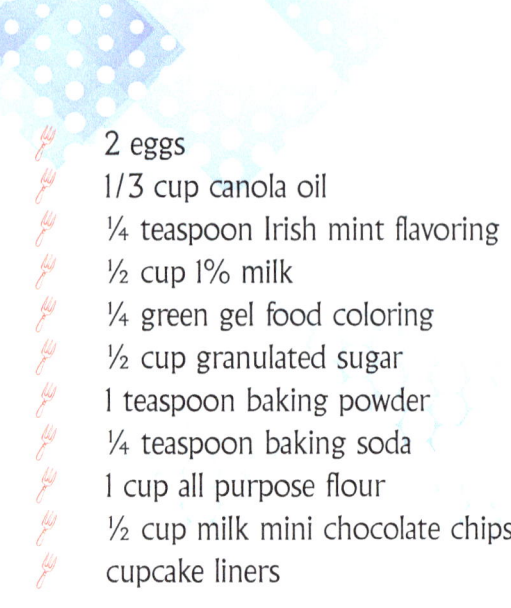

- 2 eggs
- 1/3 cup canola oil
- ¼ teaspoon Irish mint flavoring
- ½ cup 1% milk
- ¼ green gel food coloring
- ½ cup granulated sugar
- 1 teaspoon baking powder
- ¼ teaspoon baking soda
- 1 cup all purpose flour
- ½ cup milk mini chocolate chips
- cupcake liners

Preheat the oven to 350 degrees. In a mixing bowl add eggs, oil, flavoring, milk, food coloring, sugar, baking powder, baking soda, mix. Add all the flour and mix. Add the chocolate chips mix in with a spoon. Add a full ¼ cup of batter to each cupcake liner. Bake for 25 to 30 minutes.

Original Chocolate Irish Buttercream for Filling

- 4 cups confectionery sugar
- 2 sticks softened unsalted butter
- 3 tablespoons unsweetened cocoa
- ¼ teaspoon Irish mint flavoring
- 4 to 5 tablespoons 1% milk

In a mixing bowl add sugar, butter, cocoa, flavoring, start to mix on low speed adding the milk a tablespoon at a time until you get a desired consistency.

Original Irish Mint Buttercream for Top

- 9 cups confectionery sugar
- 2 sticks softened unsalted butter
- 1/8 teaspoon hobbyland Irish mint flavoring
- 1/8 teaspoon Americolor mint green gel food coloring
- 7 to 8 tablespoons 1% milk

In a mixing bowl add sugar, butter, flavoring, food coloring, mix on low speed adding the milk a tablespoon at a time to get the desired consistency.

Gluten Free & Dairy Free Chocolate Cake

- 2 eggs
- ¾ cups unsweetened original almond milk
- 1/3 cup canola oil
- 2/3 cups unsweetened cocoa
- 1 ½ cups granulated sugar
- 1 ½ teaspoons Baker's Corner baking powder or Stop & Shop baking powder
- 2 teaspoons Baker's Corner baking soda or Stop & Shop baking soda
- 1 ½ cups gluten free flour, (not the all purpose gluten free flour)
- 2/3 cups boiling water
- 9" cake pans of 2
- wax paper
- Pam nonstick cooking spray

Preheat oven to 350 degrees. In a mixing bowl add eggs, milk, oil, cocoa, sugar, baking powder, baking soda, flour, mix just until combined. Add the boiling water slowly on low speed, mix until combined. Tear a piece of wax paper off bigger then the cake pan. Lay the cake pan down on the wax paper draw a circle around the bottom of the pan, cut the circle out. Spray the bottom and the sides of the cake pan with the nonstick cooking spray. Lay the wax paper you just cut out on the bottom of the cake pan spray lightly with the nonstick cooking spray, do this for both pans. Pour the batter into both cake pans evenly, level the batter out. Bake for 20 to 25 minutes cool completely.

Gluten Free & Dairy Free Chocolate Buttercream Frosting

- 4 cups confectionery sugar
- 2 sticks softened Earth Balance Vegan butter
- 4 tablespoons unsweetened cocoa
- 3 to 4 tablespoons unsweetened original almond milk

In a mixing bowl cream together the sugar, butter, cocoa, adding the milk on low speed one tablespoon at a time until your frosting is at a desired consistency.

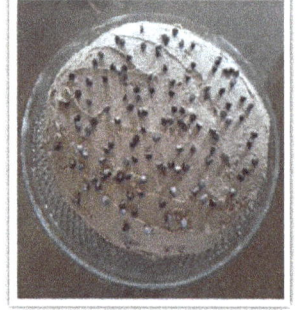

Original Chocolate Cake

- 2 eggs
- ¾ cups 1% milk or whole milk
- 1/3 cup canola oil
- 2/3 cups unsweetened cocoa
- 1 ½ cups granulated sugar
- 1 ½ teaspoons baking powder
- 2 teaspoons baking soda
- 1 ½ cups all purpose flour
- 2/3 cups boiling water
- 9" cake pans of 2
- wax paper
- nonstick cooking spray

Preheat oven to 350 degrees. In a mixing bowl add eggs, milk, oil, cocoa, sugar, baking powder, baking soda, flour, mix just until combined. Add the boiling water slowly on low speed, mix until combined. Tear a piece of wax paper off bigger then the cake pan. Lay the cake pan down on the wax paper draw a circle around the bottom of the pan, cut the circle out. Spray the bottom and the sides of the cake pan with the nonstick cooking spray. Lay the wax paper you just cut out on the bottom of the cake pan spray lightly with the nonstick cooking spray, do this for both pans. Pour the batter into both cake pans evenly, level the batter out. Bake for 20 to 25 minutes cool completely.

Original Chocolate Buttercream Frosting

- 4 cups confectionery sugar
- 2 sticks softened unsalted butter
- 4 tablespoons unsweetened cocoa
- 3 to 4 tablespoons 1% milk or whole milk

In a mixing bowl cream together the sugar, butter, cocoa, adding the milk on low speed one tablespoon at a time until your frosting is at a desired consistency.

Gluten Free & Dairy Free Homemade Custard

- 8 whole eggs
- ¾ cup granulated sugar
- 3 ½ cups unsweetened original almond milk
- 2 teaspoons freshly grated nutmeg or ground nutmeg, reserve 1 teaspoon for the top
- ½ tablespoon vanilla bean paste
- Pam nonstick cooking spray only

Preheat the oven to 350 degrees. In a large mixing bowl add the eggs and sugar whisk to combine. Add one cup of milk whisk, add the rest of the milk, whisk until all the ingredients come together. Add 1 teaspoon nutmeg, add vanilla bean paste, and whisk. Spray a glass baking dish with Pam nonstick cooking spray lightly. Pour batter in a glass baking dish. Grate 1 teaspoon freshly ground nutmeg over the top. Bake for 1 hour and 5 minutes. Take out let cool.

Note: I use ½ tablespoon of freshly grated nutmeg, depends on your taste how much to use.

Original Homemade Custard

- 8 whole eggs
- ¾ cup granulated sugar
- 3 ½ cups 1% milk
- 2 teaspoons freshly grated nutmeg or ground nutmeg, reserve 1 teaspoon for the top
- ½ tablespoon vanilla bean paste

Preheat the oven to 350 degrees. In a large mixing bowl add the eggs and sugar whisk to combine. Add one cup of milk whisk, add the rest of the milk, whisk until all the ingredients come together. Add 1 teaspoon nutmeg, add vanilla bean paste, and whisk. Spray a glass baking dish with Pam nonstick cooking spray lightly. Pour batter in a glass baking dish. Grate 1 teaspoon freshly ground nutmeg over the top. Bake for 1 hour and 5 minutes. Take out let cool.

Note: I use ½ tablespoon of freshly grated nutmeg, depends on your taste how much to use.

Gluten Free & Dairy Free Chocolate Chip Coconut Cookies

- 2 eggs
- ¾ cup granulated sugar
- 2 tablespoons light brown sugar
- 6 tablespoons Earth Balance Vegan butter
- 1 teaspoon Baker's Corner baking soda or Stop & Shop baking soda
- 1 ½ cups gluten free flour, (not the all purpose gluten free flour)
- ¾ cup Enjoy Life Semi-sweet mini chocolate chips
- ½ cup shredded sweetened coconut
- Pam nonstick cooking spray

Preheat the oven to 300 degrees. In a mixing bowl add eggs, granulated sugar, light brown sugar, butter, baking soda, mix. Add all the flour and mix. Add the chocolate chips and the coconut to the batter and mix in with a spoon. Spray a cookie sheet with a non stick cooking spray. Drop by teaspoonfuls of cookie dough onto the cookie sheet bake for 25 to 30 minutes.

Original Chocolate Chip Coconut Cookies

- 2 eggs
- ¾ cup granulated sugar
- 2 tablespoons light brown sugar
- 6 tablespoons softened unsalted butter
- 1 teaspoon baking soda
- 1 ½ cups all purpose flour
- ¾ cup milk chocolate chips
- ½ cup shredded sweetened coconut
- nonstick cooking spray

Preheat the oven to 300 degrees. In a mixing bowl add eggs, granulated sugar, light brown sugar, butter, baking soda, mix. Add all the flour and mix. Add the chocolate chips and the coconut to the batter and mix in with a spoon. Spray a cookie sheet with a non stick cooking spray. Drop by teaspoonfuls of cookie dough onto the cookie sheet bake for 25 to 30 minutes.

Gluten Free & Dairy Free Jaffa Cakes

- 2 eggs
- 1 egg white
- 1/3 cup granulated sugar
- 1/3 cup sifted gluten free flour, (not the all purpose gluten free flour)
- 1 stick softened Earth Balance Vegan butter
- 6 cup jumbo muffin tin

Preheat the oven to 350 degrees. In a mixing bowl add eggs, egg white, sugar, whip on high to incorporate the air into the ingredients for 6 minutes. Add the sifted flour and fold into the ingredients carefully. Butter the muffin tin with butter only. Add about a ¼ cup to each section. Bake for 11 minutes, take out cool completely before removing any cakes.

Directions for melting chocolate

- 1 ½ cups EnjoyLife Mini chips Semi-Sweet

Add chocolate chips to a microwave bowl. Microwave for 30 seconds at a time until smooth.

Note: Make sure when you spoon the melted chocolate over the jello the chocolate is some what cooled or it will melt your jello I use strawberry or orange which is good.

Directions for putting Jaffa cakes together

Cut rounds out of the jello make sure the rounds are smaller then the Jaffa cake. Place the jello round on the cake. Spoon the melted chocolate over the top of the jello. Put in the refrigerator to set up.

Original Jaffa Cakes

- 2 eggs
- 1 egg white
- 1/3 cup granulated sugar
- 1/3 cup sifted all purpose flour
- 1 stick softened unsalted butter
- 6 cup jumbo muffin tin

Preheat the oven to 350 degrees. In a mixing bowl add eggs, egg white, sugar, whip on high to incorporate the air into the ingredients for 6 minutes. Add the sifted flour and fold into the ingredients carefully. Butter the muffin tin with butter only. Add about a ¼ cup to each section. Bake for 11 minutes, take out cool completely before removing any cakes.

Directions for melting Chocolate

- 1 ½ cups milk or sem-sweet chocolate

Add chocolate chips to a microwave bowl. Microwave for 30 seconds at a time until smooth.

Note: Make sure when you spoon the melted chocolate over the jello the chocolate is some what cooled or it will melt your jello. I use strawberry or orange which is good.

Directions for putting Jaffa cakes together

Cut rounds out of the jello make sure the rounds are smaller then the Jaffa cake. Place the jello round on the cake. Spoon the melted chocolate over the top of the jello. Put in the refrigerator to set up.

Gluten Free and Dairy Free Christmas Sugar Cookies

- 1 egg
- ½ cup granulated sugar
- ½ cup confectionery sugar
- 2 tablespoons softened Earth Balance Vegan butter
- ½ teaspoon to 1 teaspoon almond extract
- ½ teaspoon cream of tarter
- ½ teaspoon Bakers Corner baking soda or Stop & Shop baking soda
- 1 ¼ cup gluten free flour, (not the all purpose gluten free flour)
- ½ cup gluten free all purpose flour

Preheat oven to 300 degrees. In a mixing bowl add egg, granulated sugar, confectionery sugar, butter, almond extract, cream of tartar, baking soda and mix. Add the flour a little at a time, mix just until combined. Make dough into a ball wrap in plastic wrap, put into the refrigerator at least 20 minutes. Before rolling the dough out sprinkle confectionery sugar down on the service roll out, start to cut your shapes out with a Christmas cookie cutter. Spray the cookie sheet with Pam (Original nonstick cooking spray only). Place your cookies on the cookie sheet and bake for 15 minutes, take out and transfer to a cooling rack.

Gluten Free and Dairy Free Buttercream Frosting For The Cookies

- 8 tablespoons softened Earth Balance Vegan butter
- 2 ½ cups confectionery sugar
- 5 ½ tablespoons water or unsweetened vanilla almond milk

In a mixing bowl add the butter and sugar adding the water or milk a little at a time.

Original Christmas Sugar Cookie

- 1 egg
- 2 tablespoons water
- ½ cup granulated sugar
- ½ cup confectionery sugar
- 2 tablespoons softened unsalted butter
- ½ teaspoon to 1 teaspoon almond extract
- ½ teaspoon cream of tarter
- ½ teaspoon baking soda
- 1 ¼ cup all purpose flour

Preheat oven to 300 degrees. In a mixing bowl add egg, water, granulated sugar, confectionery sugar, butter, almond extract, cream of tartar, baking soda and mix. Add the flour a little at a time, mix just until combined. Make dough into a ball wrap in plastic wrap, put into the refrigerator at least 20 minutes. Roll your cookies on a floured service with a rolling pin, then start to cut your shapes out with a Christmas cookie cutter. Spray your cookie sheet with a nonstick cooking spray. Place your cookie cut outs on the cookie sheet and bake for 15 to 20 minutes, transfer to a cooling rack.

Buttercream Frosting For the Cookies

- 8 tablespoons softened unsalted butter
- 2 ½ cups confectionery sugar
- 5 ½ teaspoon water or 1% milk

In a mixing bowl add the butter and sugar mix adding the water or milk a little at a time.

Gluten Free & Dairy Free Coconut Cupcakes

- 2 eggs
- ½ cup granulated sugar
- 1/3 cup canola oil
- ½ cup unsweetened original almond milk
- ½ teaspoon hobbyland coconut flavoring
- 1 teaspoon Baker's Corner baking powder or Stop & Shop baking powder
- ¼ teaspoon Baker's Corner baking soda or Stop & Shop baking soda
- 1 cup gluten free flour, (not the all purpose gluten free flour)
- cupcake liners
- Pam non-stick cooking spray

Preheat oven to 350 degrees. In a mixing bowl add eggs, sugar, oil, milk, flavoring, baking powder, baking soda and mix. Add all the flour and mix just until combined. Add a full ¼ cup of batter to each cupcake liner bake for 20 to 25 minutes.

Note: You don't want to add wet pineapple on to the buttercream.

Gluten Free & Dairy Free Pina Colada Buttercream

- 3 cups confectionery sugar
- 1 ½ sticks softened Earth Balance Vegan butter
- ½ teaspoon Pina Colada flavoring
- 3 tablespoons unsweetened original almond milk
- shredded coconut
- chunked pineapple drained and pat with a paper towel

In a mixing bowl add the sugar, butter, flavoring, adding the milk a tablespoon at a time. Mix on high for 20 seconds. Frost your cooled cupcakes then sprinkle with coconut and add a chunk of pineapple on the top.

Original Coconut Cupcakes

- 2 eggs
- ½ cup granulated sugar
- 1/3 cup canola oil
- ½ cup 1% milk
- ½ teaspoon hobbyland coconut flavoring
- 1 teaspoon baking powder
- ¼ teaspoon baking soda
- 1 cup all purpose flour
- cupcake liners
- non-stick cooking spray

Preheat oven to 350 degrees. In a mixing bowl add eggs, sugar, oil, milk, flavoring, baking powder, baking soda and mix. Add all the flour and mix just until combined. Add a full ¼ cup of batter to each cupcake liner bake for 20 to 25 minutes.

Note: You don't want to add wet pineapple on to the buttercream.

Original Pina Colada Buttercream

- 3 cups confectionery sugar
- 1 ½ sticks softened unsalted butter
- ½ teaspoon Pina Colada flavoring
- 3 tablespoons 1% milk
- shredded coconut
- chunked pineapple

In a mixing bowl add the sugar, butter, flavoring, adding the milk a tablespoon at a time. Mix on high for 20 seconds. Frost your cooled cupcakes then sprinkle with coconut and add a chunk of pineapple on the top.

Gluten Free & Dairy Free Red Velvet Cupcakes

- 2/3 cup unsweetened original almond milk
- 2 teaspoons cold white vinegar

In a glass bowl add milk and vinegar, mix. Let set for 5 minutes stirring before adding into the bowl.

- 2 eggs
- ½ cup granulated sugar
- 2 tablespoons unsweetened cocoa
- 1 tablespoon Americolor red food coloring
- 1/3 cup canola oil
- 1 teaspoon Baker's Corner baking powder or Stop & Shop baking powder
- ¼ teaspoon Baker's Corner baking soda or Stop & Shop baking soda
- 1 cup gluten free flour, (not the all purpose gluten free flour)
- cupcake liners

Preheat oven to 350 degrees. In a mixing bowl add the milk and vinegar mixture, eggs, sugar, cocoa, food coloring, oil, baking powder, baking soda and mix. Add all the flour and mix. Add a full ¼ cup of batter to each cupcake liner. Bake for 25 to 30 minutes.

Note: If you want to make just the buttercream leave out the French vanilla flavoring.

Gluten Free & Dairy Free Buttercream or Gluten Free & Dairy Free French Vanilla Buttercream

- 4 cups confectionery sugar
- 2 sticks softened Earth Balance Vegan Butter
- 3 to 4 unsweetened original almond milk
- ½ teaspoon French vanilla flavoring, optional

In a mixing bowl add all the sugar, butter. Start the mixer on low speed adding the milk a tablespoon at a time. Mix on high for 20 seconds or longer. This will incorporate air into the frosting to make it white and fluffy.

Original Red Velvet Cupcakes

- 2/3 cup 1% milk
- 2 teaspoons white vinegar

In a glass bowl add the milk and vinegar, let set for 5 minute. Stirring before adding to the mixing bowl.

- 2 eggs
- ½ cup granulated sugar
- 1 teaspoon baking powder
- ¼ teaspoon baking soda
- 2 level tablespoons unsweetened cocoa
- 1 tablespoon Americolor red food coloring
- ½ cup canola oil
- 1 cup all purpose flour
- cupcake liners

Preheat the oven to 350 degrees. In a mixing bowl add the milk and vinegar mixture, eggs, sugar, baking powder, baking soda, cocoa, food coloring, oil and mix. Add all the flour and mix. Add a full ¼ cup of batter to the cupcake liners bake for 25 to 30 minutes.

Note: If you want to make just the buttercream leave out the French vanilla flavoring.

Original Buttercream or French Vanilla Buttercream

- 4 cups confectionery sugar
- 2 sticks softened unsalted butter
- 3 to 4 tablespoons 1% milk
- ½ teaspoon French vanilla flavoring, optional

In a mixing bowl add all the sugar, butter. Start the mixer on low speed adding the milk a tablespoon at a time. Mix on high for 20 seconds or longer. This will incorporate air into the frosting to make it white and fluffy.

Gluten Free & Dairy Free Strudel Topping Mini Cinnamon Breads

- 2 eggs
- 1 tablespoon canola oil
- ½ cup applesauce
- ½ cup original almond milk
- ½ cup granulated sugar
- ¼ cup light brown sugar
- 1 teaspoon ground cinnamon
- 1 teaspoon Baker's Corner baking powder or Stop & Shop baking powder
- ¼ teaspoon Baker's Corner baking powder or Stop & Shop baking soda
- 1 cup gluten free flour, (not the all purpose gluten free flour)
- non-stick mini loaf pan, 8 cavity or a 6 cup mini loaf pan

Preheat the oven to 350 degrees. In a mixing bowl add eggs, oil, applesauce, almond milk, granulated sugar, light brown sugar, cinnamon, baking powder, baking soda and mix. Add the flour all at once mix on high just until the batter looks smooth. Add a ½ cup of batter to each section you may only get 6 mini breads doing it this way. Recipe is below for the strudel make the strudel and cover the tops of the breads with this mixture before baking. Bake for 25 to 30 minutes.

Note: You can make these smaller to get 8 mini breads.

Strudel Topping

- ½ cup light brown sugar
- 3 tablespoons softened Earth Balance Vegan butter
- ½ cup gluten free oatmeal
- 1/8 teaspoon ground cinnamon
- ½ teaspoon gluten free flour, (not the all purpose gluten free flour)
- ½ cup chopped walnuts, optional

In a glass bowl add brown sugar, butter, oatmeal, cinnamon and flour mix together. I cover the tops of the breads with this strudel.

Original Strudel Topping Mini Cinnamon Breads

- 2 eggs
- 1 tablespoon canola oil
- ½ cup applesauce
- ½ cup milk
- ½ cup granulated sugar
- ¼ cup light brown sugar
- 1 teaspoon ground cinnamon
- 1 teaspoon baking powder
- ¼ teaspoon baking soda
- 1 cup all purpose flour
- non-stick mini loaf pan, 8 cavity or a 6 cup mini loaf pan

Preheat the oven to 350 degrees. In a mixing bowl add eggs, oil, applesauce, milk, granulated sugar, light brown sugar, cinnamon, baking powder, baking soda and mix. Add the flour all at once mix on high just until the batter looks smooth. Add a ½ cup of batter to each section you may only get 6 mini breads doing it this way. Recipe is below for the strudel make the strudel and cover the tops of the breads with this mixture before baking. Bake for 25 to 30 minutes.

Note: You can make these smaller to get 8 mini breads or use the 6 mini loaf pan.

Strudel Topping

- ½ cup light brown sugar
- 3 tablespoons softened unsalted butter
- ½ cup original oatmeal
- 1/8 teaspoon ground cinnamon
- ½ teaspoon all purpose flour
- ½ cup chopped walnuts, optional

In a glass bowl add brown sugar, butter, oatmeal, cinnamon and flour mix together. I cover the tops of the breads with this strudel.

Gluten Free & Dairy Free Snicker Doodle Cookies

- 2 eggs
- 3 tablespoons softened Earth Balance Vegan butter
- ½ cup light brown sugar
- ½ cup granulated sugar
- 1 teaspoon cream of tarter
- 1 teaspoon Baker's Corner baking soda or Stop & Shop baking soda
- 1 teaspoon cinnamon
- 1 ½ cups gluten free flour, (not the all purpose gluten free flour)
- Pam nonstick cooking spray

Preheat oven to 300 degrees. In a mixing bowl add eggs, butter, brown sugar, granulated sugar, cream of tarter, baking soda, cinnamon and mix. Add all the flour and mix. Spray the cookie sheet generously. Drop the cookie dough by teaspoonfuls onto the cookie sheet. Bake for 25 to 30 minutes.

Original Snicker Doodle Cookies

- 2 eggs
- 3 tablespoons softened unsalted butter
- ½ cup light brown sugar
- ½ cup granulated sugar
- 1 teaspoon cream of tarter
- 1 teaspoon baking soda
- 1 teaspoon cinnamon
- 1 ½ cups all purpose flour
- nonstick cooking spray

Preheat oven to 300 degrees. In a mixing bowl add eggs, butter, brown sugar, granulated sugar, cream of tarter, baking soda, cinnamon and mix. Add all the flour and mix. Spray the cookie sheet generously. Drop the cookie dough by teaspoonfuls onto the cookie sheet. Bake for 25 to 30 minutes.

Gluten Free and Dairy Free Peanut Butter Cups

- 1/3 cup gluten free smooth peanut butter
- 1/8 teaspoon sea salt or table salt
- 1 tablespoon confectionery sugar
- 1 cup Enjoy Life Semi-sweet Vegan chocolate chips
- cupcake liners

In a glass measuring cup add peanut butter, salt, sugar set aside. In a glass measuring cup or a glass microwave bowl add 1 cup chocolate chips. Add the chocolate chips to the microwave for 30 seconds at a time stirring in between. Mix the chocolate until smooth. Put the peanut butter mixture in the microwave for 15 to 20 seconds, take out mix until smooth. Take a cupcake paper and add 1 teaspoon chocolate to the bottom and spread half way up the sides and cover the bottom. Add ½ tablespoon of the peanut butter mixture to the center spread a little. Add a half of a tablespoon for the top and spread. Put into the refrigerator for 20 minutes to set up.

Original Peanut Butter Cups

- 1/3 cup smooth peanut butter
- 1/8 teaspoon sea salt
- 1 tablespoon confectionery sugar
- 2 cups semi-sweet chocolate chips or milk chocolate or white chocolate
- Cupcake papers

In a glass measuring cup add peanut butter, salt, sugar set aside. In a glass measuring cup or a glass microwave bowl add 1 cup chocolate chips. Add the chocolate chips to the microwave for 30 seconds at a time mixing in between. Put the peanut butter mixture in the microwave for 15 to 20 seconds, take out mix until smooth. Take a cupcake paper and add ½ tablespoon of melted chocolate spread on the bottom and half way up the sides. Take ½ tablespoon of the peanut butter filling place in the middle spread a little. Now for the top take ½ tablespoon of melted chocolate or a little more over the top and spread. Put the peanut butter cups on a plate and put into the refrigerator for 20 minutes.

Microwaves: If you have an older microwave this will work differently then a new one on how the chocolate chips melt.

Bonus Recipe For Gluten Free Turkey Gravy

- 5 tablespoons Earth Balance Vegan butter
- 3 cups fat free turkey broth
- ½ cup gluten free flour, (not the all purpose gluten free flour)
- salt & pepper to your taste

In your pot add the 5 tablespoons of butter let melt a little, add all the flour whisk cook for 3 seconds or so. Turn the heat up on medium high add all the broth and whisk slowly until smooth and thickened take off the heat.

Note: You can use canned or boxed Turkey or chicken broth. When making this gravy you need to keep mixing. The gluten free flour settles to the bottom of the pot this will burn.

Tip: If you don't bake your turkey the night before you can always boil up the tail the neck. On the back side of the turkey just cut the extra skin off the back you can get some kind of broth out of these parts.

Gluten Free and Dairy Free Chocolate Pudding or Hot Chocolate

- ½ cup original unsweetened almond milk
- 4 tablespoons cornstarch
- 2 cups original unsweetened almond milk
- 3 tablespoons granulated sugar
- 1/3 cup Enjoy Life chocolate chips

You will need a heavy bottom pot. In a container with a tight fitting lid add the ½ cup almond milk and 4 tablespoons cornstarch shake and set aside. Add to the pot almond milk, sugar 1/3 cup chocolate chips. Turn the heat to medium shaking the cornstarch mixture adding to the pot, whisking until thick. Take off the heat add a ½ cup of the chocolate chips and whisk or stir until melted. Put the pudding into dessert dishes let sit at room temperature for 6 minutes then put a piece of plastic right on to the pudding so this does not form a skin put into the refrigerator to cool.

Note: You can skip the cornstarch step and have this for a hot cup of cocoa. If your a chocolate lover you can add more chocolate chips.

Ingredient Information

Gluten Free Food Additives

FD&C Blue No. 1 Dye
- FD&C Blue No. 1 Lake
- FD&C Blue No. 2 Dye
- FD&C Blue No. 2 Lake
- FD&C Green No. 3 Dye
- FD&C Green No. 3 Lake
- FD&C Red No. 3 Dye
- FD&C Red No. 40 Dye
- FD&C Red No. 40 Lake
- FD&C Yellow No. 5 Dye
- FD&C Yellow No. 6 Dye
- FD&C Yellow No. 6 Lake
- http://www.foodadditivesworld.com/articles/gluten-free.html

Peanut Delight Natural Creamy peanut butter—You can buy this at Aldi's grocery store it is low sodium and is gluten free and lactose free.

Tofutti—This imitation cream cheese by Tofutti is a milk free and kosher alternative to traditional cream cheese. Every 8-ounce tub of this bulk food item is free of gluten, trans fat, cholesterol, sugar, butterfat, animal derivatives, hydrogenated oils, and lactose. Tofutti's "Better Than Cream Cheese" is also low in carbohydrates.

Food coloring—If you run out of red food coloring and you have metallic red food paint that works just as well as red food coloring. Or you can use Chef Master neon brite pink, with the cocoa in the batter this will make the pink look like red. Chef Master food coloring you can buy at Amazon.com

Paint Metallic (rainbow dust) all colors—Are gluten free

Maraschino Cherries natural NON-GMO project verified, natural color, no perservatives, gluten free, vegan kosher, fat free.

The modern **maraschino cherry** is soaked in a salt brine or—even worse—a solution of calcium chloride and sulfur dioxide. This bleaches the cherries, removing their natural color and flavoring. They are then pitted and soaked in a sweetener (typically high fructose corn syrup or HFCS) for about a month.

Cream of tarter—Contains only one ingredient tartaric acid which is found in certain types of fruit. Cream of tarter is safe to eat if you have a milk allergy.

Vivian's creamy whipped Topping Soy and Dairy free-available at amazon.com

Enjoy Life Mini Chocolate Chips—Verified NON-GMO, Allergy-friendly, Certified, gluten free, Vegan, Kosher, Halal, Pateo-friendly. Enjoy Life products are free from gluten and wheat, peanuts, dairy, tree nuts, soy, casein, sulfites, egg, lupin, sesame, fish, mustard, crustaceans, shell fish.

Pure sugar is gluten-free. Most **suga**r comes either from **sugar** beets or from **sugar** cane. Even though **sugar** cane is a grass plant **and** therefore a distant relative to the **gluten** grains **wheat**, barley, **and** rye, it does not contain the harmful gluten protein.

Brown sugar is also **gluten-free.** It is made by taking plain white sugar and mixing it with molasses, which is **gluten-free.** Molasses is made either from sugar beets or sugarcane, much the same as crystallized **sugar**.

Wintergreen Flavor Extract is vegan, kosher, and **gluten-free**.

By its nature, **baking powder** is **gluten-free** because it doesn't have wheat, rye, barley, or triticale, the four types of grains that contain the protein.Oct 2, 2019

Libby's 100% pumpkin is gluten free and all natural

Rumfords baking powder is aluminum free and gluten free

Earth Balance Vegan butter sticks are gluten free and dairy free and all natural

Pascha organic white baking chips

How bad is soy lecithin for you?

Soy lecithin is used as an additive to enhance flavor and make foods seem creamier. Because soy lecithin is so highly processed, it's unlikely to contain any gluten, Jul 13, 2017

Is soy lecithin the same as soy?

Soybeans are well—recognized as allergenic foods. ...Soy lecithin does contain trace levels of soy proteins and these have been found to include soy allergens. However, apparently, soy lecithin does not contain sufficient soy protein residues to provoke allergic reactions in the majority of soy-allergic consumers.

Bananas—Use the bananas when they are pale or brown best for baking. If you don't use the bananas right away put them in a freezer bag and freeze them until your ready to use them.

Cool Whip—Does contain 2% of cream. A lot of whip topping have sodium caseinate which is cows milk that has been converted into sodium caseinate. People who have milk allergies read the labels carefully.

Substitutions

As long as there is enough of an acidic ingredients reaction (for a ½ teaspoon baking soda, you will need 1 cup of buttermilk or yogurt or 1 teaspoon lemon juice or vinegar) And remember that baking soda has 4 times the power of baking powder, a ¼ teaspoon baking soda is equivalent to 1 teaspoon of baking powder

Substitute for a mashed banana—1 tablespoon canola oil, 1 tablespoon olive oil or coconut oil or replace half the amount of oil for mashed bananas in baking adjust if you need to. 1 Cup vegetable oil substitute ½ cup applesauce or fruit puree. Use half applesauce and half fat.

Substitute for mayonnaise—You can use sour cream or yogurt in most recipes

Substitute for eggs—Egg beaters or 1 ½ tablespoons vegetable oil and 1 ½ tablespoons of water with 1 teaspoon baking powder per egg. This is for a substitute for one egg if you see 2 eggs just double.

Gluten-Free Baking Substitutes

All-Purpose Gluten-Free Flour. Brands such as Bob's Red Mill and Robin Hood's Nutri Flour blend are among the most popular and will serve your baking requirements on a basic level.

- Hazelnut Flour. ...
- Buckwheat Flour. ...
- Quinoa Flour. ...
- **Coconut Flour.** ...

Replace **gluten,** you'll need to use other thickeners like xanthan gum or guar gum in your **baking.** For each cup of **gluten-free flour mix,** add at least 1 teaspoon of **gluten substitute.**

Almond Flour

One cup of almond **flour** contains about 90 almonds and has a nutty flavor. It's commonly used in baked goods and can be a grain-**free alternative** to breadcrumbs. It can typically be substituted in a 1:1 ratio in place of **regular** or **wheat flour.** If you are baking with this type of **flour,** use one extra egg.

If you need to **substitute flour:**

When cooking **gluten-free**, it's not always a cup-for-cup replacement. ... Almond flour: substitute 1:1 with all-purpose (white) flour. Note: **Almond flour** typically requires more egg or binding agent, so the recipe might need to be altered.

Most store—bought **gluten-free all-purpose flour** mixes are about 1:1 for **all-purpose flour,** So, **if** your **recipe** calls for 2 cups of **all-purpose flour, you can substitute** 2 cups of the **gluten-free flour.**

Substitution for 1 teaspoon baking powder—¼ teaspoon baking soda, ½ teaspoon cream of tarter, ¼ teaspoon cornstarch

Substitution for 2 teaspoons baking powder—½ teaspoon baking soda, 1 teaspoon cream of tarter, ¼ teaspoon cornstarch

Allergen information—AmeriColor Corp.

Peanuts: NO Tree Nuts: NO Powdered Egg Whites: MERINGUE POWDER Dairy or Dairy Derivative: NO Soy or Soy Derivative: CANDY COLOR *Gluten*: NO

There is no gluten in AmeriColor products.

Author Biography

I love reading my bible each day, I love my husband he is my rock, I love horse back riding, fishing, swimming, boating, baking, cooking. As I was growing up my brothers and I did all these activities. Family is so important to me we love getting together when we can. I love people, I am a people person. Everyone that knows me knows this all to well. I love all the cooking and baking. I started baking when my mom bought me an easy bake oven my mom taught everything I needed to know about cooking and baking. My favorite Holiday is Christmas, I love the Christmas lights and everything that goes with Christmas. I love snowmen I have a great collection. Everyday to me is such a Blessing because tomorrow is not promised to any of us.

My Dedication to My Mom

My mom taught me everything about cooking and baking. I was always in the kitchen with her when she was cooking the smells were so good and yummy. She always took the time out to answer any questions I had and showed me my mistakes so I could improve. I would not be where I am today if it was not for her. I just want to let her know this is all because of her and I love her with all my heart.

www.ingramcontent.com/pod-product-compliance
Lightning Source LLC
Chambersburg PA
CBHW061105070526
44579CB00011B/143